BUS

A PORTFOLIO OF

HOME SPA
IDEAS

COWLES
Creative Publishing

CONTENTS

© Copyright 1998
Cowles Creative Publishing, Inc.
5900 Green Oak Drive
Minnetonka, Minnesota 55343
1-800-328-3895

Printed in U.S.A.
Library of Congress
Cataloging-in-Publication Data
A portfolio of home spa ideas.
        p. cm.
    ISBN 0-86573-890-4
    1. Spa pools. 2. Hot tubs. I. Cowles Creative Publishing.
TH4761.P67 1998
690'.896--dc21   98-17225

Associate Creative Director: Tim Himsel
Editorial Director: Bryan Trandem
Managing Editor: Jennifer Caliandro
Project Manager: Michelle Skudlarek
Writer: Carol Harvatin
Editor: Carolyn Witthuhn
Art Directors: Todd Sauers, Brad Webster
Copy Editor: Janice Cauley
Vice President of Development
    Planning & Production: Jim Bindas
Production Manager: Kim Gerber

Printed on American paper by R. R. Donnelley & Sons Co.

President: Iain Macfarlane
Group Director, Book Development: Zoe Graul
Creative Director: Lisa Rosenthal
Senior Managing Editor: Elaine Perry
01 00 99 98 / 5 4 3 2 1

Other Portfolio of Ideas books include:

Photos on page two (top to bottom) courtesy of Kohler Co.,
Pittsburgh Corning Corp., and Mountain Hot Tubs. Photos on
page three (top to bottom) courtesy of ETS, Inc., NordicTrack, Inc.,
and Marquis Spas.

Photos on cover (clockwise) courtesy of Archadeck, National Spa
and Pool Institute, VELUX Roof Windows and Skylights, T.C.T.
Landscaping, National Spa and Pool Institute, and Finnleo Sauna
and Steam.

*You can transform any area in your home or yard into a home spa—a place conducive to exercise, relaxation, reflection, or social interaction—
like this redwood hot tub large enough for several persons to enjoy a whirling warm-water massage.*

WHY BUILD A SPA IN YOUR HOME?

For thousands of years, people have flocked to naturally-occurring hot springs, seeking the relaxing and therapeutic benefits of warm, swirling water. In the past, enterprising individuals tapped into these springs, developing them into luxurious resorts. Today, exclusive spas and resorts continue to thrive. Even hotels, realizing the attraction of spas, have installed hot tubs, treadmills, and saunas for weary travelers.

Homeowners have taken notice and are creating their own spas in backyards, bedrooms, or basements. Why? Because more people than ever are making a commitment to good health and physical well-being. For some, this means regular workouts, followed by a cleansing steam bath. Others relieve stress and muscle tension in the whirling water of a spa tub or whirlpool. Some prefer the dry heat of a sauna, while others escape into tanning booths, health environment capsules, or environmental enclosures. If you'd like to revitalize your lifestyle, a customized home spa might be just what you're looking for.

The term "spa" has become a catchall phrase representing everything from pulsating shower heads to exclusive health resorts. In this book, we define "home spa" as a personal space in your home or yard that is conducive to exercise, relaxation, reflection, and social interaction.

A Portfolio of Home Spa Ideas will inspire you with ideas for turning any area in your home into a personal spa. It will set you on your way to creating a home spa suited to your taste and needs by helping you to determine who will use it, elements you may want to include, the amount of money you want to spend, and where you want to place it.

Popular items in home spas include jetted tubs, saunas, steam baths, and exercise equipment, along with other innovations that enhance and promote a healthy lifestyle. Existing electrical and plumbing systems will need to be inspected to ensure your home can handle the components you want.

The aesthetic atmosphere you create is the final detail in making your home spa complete. Throughout this book, you'll find ideas for creating a special ambience in your spa, from scented candles in a bath with a whirlpool tub to exercise areas with mirrored walls and music.

The Portfolio section examines the various functions of home spas—spas for relaxation, spas for socializing, spas that enhance physical well-being, and multifunctional combination spas that offer a complete selection of spa options in one sensational space.

A Portfolio of Home Spa Ideas will show you how to choose and coordinate the right combination of elements to create a home spa that will take you away from your hectic life without your ever leaving the house.

BENEFITS OF A HOME SPA

Why build a spa in your home? The primary benefits—relaxation, recreation or socialization, and health—often overlap.

Spas provide a place to relax. Who hasn't soaked in a warm bath at the end of a long day or after a vigorous workout? Heat and water therapy are good for the mind and the body. In addition to the warm water, strategically placed jets in whirlpools and hot tubs massage different parts of the body, providing total relaxation. Many families unwind by relaxing in a steamy whirlpool or spa tub after a long day at the office or a rough day on the football field. A spa provides a place for total solitude and relaxation, a refuge from our hectic life, where we can

regroup, revitalize, and forget about the minor problems of the day—at least for a while.

Spas expand recreational or leisure activities. Groups of people have always gathered and socialized at watering holes, from swimming pools to lakes to the ocean. With a spa, you can spend quality time with friends and family, engaging in friendly conversation while enjoying a satisfying soak. Some people choose to spend an evening soaking in a hot tub rather than going to a movie or play. They may even invite friends over, making it a special or party occasion.

Health benefits of home spas are numerous, ranging from relief for aching muscles to rehabilitative massage therapy for those with

A comfortable lounge area invites you into the steam bath or the sauna to rejuvenate and refresh after a long day at the office, at school, or at play.

muscle or nerve injuries. Physical trainers long have recognized the benefits of water therapy for athletes with painful joints or sore muscles. Studies show that soaking in warm water improves circulation and is beneficial to those with arthritis or muscle pain. Hot-water bathing relieves physical stress and reduces mental stress and tension as well.

So, what are you waiting for? Adding a spa to your home will increase your ability to relax, benefit your health, and enhance your social life.

Unwind at the end of the day and spend quality time with family members in your personal home spa tub.

Home gyms that feature a variety of components allow you to exercise different parts of your body for a total body workout.

PLANNING

Begin planning your home spa by determining how you will use it. Will yours be a social spa with a large jetted tub and space for food and beverage service, towel storage, and a dressing area? Or, will your spa be a quiet, cozy whirlpool in a master bathroom for restful reflection?

Think about who will use the spa. When choosing a tub, you need to determine the average number of people that will use the spa at any one time. Will it be friends, family, or just yourself? What will their needs be? Do they need a place to change and store clothes?

What functions do you want your spa to serve? Do you want a place to rest and relax? Or a convenient place to exercise in private? Think about the aesthetic environment you want to create. Elements such as furniture, lighting, color, music, and entertainment all affect the mood you create in your home spa environment.

You'll need to consider where you want to put your home spa. Do you want to install it indoors next to your bedroom or place it outdoors on the deck? Will you need any upgrades for structure, plumbing, or electrical?

Do you have enough room for all the elements you want to include? Obviously, space constraints can affect your choice of features, but you might be surprised at the number of elements you can fit into a relatively small space. For example, to create a spa that fits your space, you can find smaller whirlpool tubs, and exercise equipment that folds up and stores away.

Another important consideration in planning a home spa is your budget. How much do you want to spend? The cost of a home spa varies, ranging from the modest cost of installing a small whirlpool tub in an existing bathtub space to the higher cost of creating a multifunctional exercise spa, complete with jetted spa tub, sauna, and exercise equipment, as well as furniture and accessories.

Photo courtesy of Finnleo Sauna and Steam

The multiple components of combination or multifunctional spas—inviting lounge area, enclosed steam bath, and well-designed sauna—offer homeowners a retreat from everyday routine.

Make your backyard deck more inviting by adding a covered freestanding hot tub.

Cathedral-style windows welcome the sun, creating openness in this spacious, modern home spa. Ample natural lighting makes a spa very inviting.

ELEMENTS OF A HOME SPA

In the planning section, you began by deciding what function your spa will perform. The next step is choosing elements that best carry out that function. For example, a relaxation spa includes jetted tubs, saunas, steam rooms, a restful atmosphere, and a comfortable place to cool down. All of these elements combine to create a spa that functions as a quiet haven for stress-relieving relaxation.

Many of these elements, such as jetted tubs, are found in all three types: relaxation spas, recreation/socialization spas, and health spas. While some elements are associated with a certain type of spa, don't allow this to limit how you use them in your spa. For example, a home gym can be used to improve your health and also as a place to socialize. People use elements in different ways for a variety of reasons.

Aesthetic factors will play a part in creating the look and feel of your home spa environment. These factors include color, lighting, furniture, stereo, television, and VCR equipment.

Photo courtesy of Nautilus International

A home gym or other exercise equipment is an essential element for a health spa.

One of the most popular elements in a home spa is an outdoor hot tub. Redwood cedar canopies stand guard over this hot tub installed in an expansive backyard deck. While this shaded pavilion is ideal for entertaining friends, it also offers a quiet space for reflection and solitude.

ELEMENTS OF A HOME SPA

In today's busy world, relaxation is a valuable commodity. Elements that promote relaxation include jetted tubs, saunas, and steam cabinets, as well as environmental enclosures and multi-faceted shower systems. Soothing colors, quiet music, and comfortable furniture are aesthetic elements that also enhance relaxation.

A huge benefit in having a home exercise spa is the convenience and practicality of a private place to work out. Good equipment is a primary element of exercise spas. As home spas become more popular, more equipment manufacturers are realizing the value of exercise equipment specially designed for in-home use. A home gym might also include bright lights, motivating music, mirrors, and exercise mats.

A home sauna is another element to include in your spa. Saunas are ideal for detoxifying your body naturally through your body's own perspiration. A well-designed space in which to cool down afterward completes the sauna experience.

If you are planning a spa where you can spend time with friends and family, make sure you have enough seating and floor space to accommodate everyone. In addition to furniture, you may want to add other elements, such as a dressing area, a workout space large enough for an aerobic workout, and a quiet, cozy corner for cooling down after a soak in a hot tub.

Other elements you can include in your home spa are personal beauty enhancements such as tanning beds, facial systems, and herbal wraps.

Saunas are available in a variety of kits that fit your space and needs. Or, you can have one built to your specifications. Some manufacturers offer kits with deluxe features, such as the notched design repeated in the built-in backrests and bench skirt of this sauna.

A large hot tub can be used to entertain friends and can be installed indoors or outdoors on the patio or deck.

Shower systems come in a variety of styles and sizes. This one contains several wall-mounted jets that you control and manipulate for a full-body water massage.

Whirlpools are available in many sizes, styles, and colors. This one features a cascade spout and faucet set in bright brass.

TYPES OF TUBS

Tubs for home spas come in two general types: whirlpool tubs and larger tubs, often called hot tubs.

Whirlpools, in general, are smaller and less expensive. They usually are installed indoors, often in an existing bathtub space. Unlike hot tubs, they don't need daily water sanitation since they are filled with water heated from your hot water heater and then drained after each use.

Hot tubs hold water *all* the time, so they must be continuously heated, circulated, filtered, and sanitized. They can be installed indoors or out.

Each type of home spa tub is available in a variety of styles, colors, and sizes, with the four-person model being the most popular. Tubs can be inset partially or completely in the floor, a deck, or the ground. Most indoor tubs are whirlpools, while outdoor tubs include a variety of styles—hot tubs, portable spas, soft-sided tubs, built-in concrete spas, and swim spas.

In spite of their differences, hot tubs and whirlpools have basically the same function—a luxurious, relaxing soak.

Photo courtesy of National Spa and Pool Institute

Water gently flowing from two pools and natural stones create a peaceful retreat for this beautifully landscaped outdoor tub.

Spa tubs can be part of a larger swimming pool. This concrete spa is the perfect place to invite neighbors and friends for a relaxing soak.

This portable spa is easy to install. Just plug it into an outlet and fill from your garden hose. Roomy enough for several people, it easily fits in smaller places.

Attractively inset in wood and ceramic tile, this hot tub takes advantage of corner windows with a view.

WHIRLPOOLS

Relaxing in a hot bath is an effective way to unwind. Whirlpools enhance this experience with comfortable molded seats and gentle, massaging water jets. With some models offering up to ten jets, whirlpools often are recommended for people suffering from chronic muscle pain or muscle-related injuries.

In their simplest form, whirlpools are nothing more than enhanced bathtubs. Whirlpool tubs circulate water mixed with air through jets mounted in the body of the tub. The pumps move the water around the tub rapidly to create a massaging effect. Installed indoors, they generally are large enough to accommodate one or two bathers comfortably.

Whirlpools come in a variety of sizes, shapes, and colors. Some are small enough to fit into the same space as a standard bathtub. Sizes range from a standard 60-inch by 30-inch rectangle to large, spacious tubs built to hold more than one bather. Drop-in models offer the best variety of shapes and sizes. Freestanding tubs are ideal for small baths.

Some whirlpools require a wooden surround or deck of some kind, which can be finished in ceramic tile or wood paneling. They usually are made of cast iron, porcelain-enamel steel, gel-coated fiberglass, or fiberglass-backed acrylic. They cost less and fit in smaller bathrooms. Because they are drained after each use (like standard tubs), they don't require daily water-sanitation maintenance. Secondary heaters are available on some models.

Whirlpools can fit in standard bathtub spaces. This one is a great replacement for a conventional bathtub.

This whirlpool bath, large enough for two bathers, features jets for lower back massage and for foot massage. An automatic in-line heater maintains water temperature.

(left) Whirlpools come in many shapes and sizes. The unique styling of this tub creates a focus for the entire bathroom.

(upper right) This corner bath allows plenty of space for stretching out and enjoying a relaxing water massage.

(lower right) With generous space for two, this circular bath is ideal for corner, platform, or island installations.

(below) This drop-in model with cascading spout is inset in a marble-tiled floor, adding luxury and elegance to the whirlpool bathing experience.

17

Whirlpools

If you are choosing a whirlpool tub as an element in your spa, consider whether you want a whirlpool for gentle warm-water relaxation or for specific hydromassage therapy. The type of whirlpool tub you choose is determined by the whirlpool effect you want.

Typical whirlpools have at least six jets. Some have jets that create swirling water for gentle relaxation. Other whirlpools have strong pulsating jets for a vigorous hydromassage. The amount of control you have over the pumps and jets will vary from tub to tub. The more options offered, the more expensive the tub.

This whirlpool's color and shape make a dramatic statement in any bath or home spa. A cascading spout completes the effect.

Stately columns framing a pastoral backdrop and comfortable chaise lounge evoke the richness and elegance of a bygone era.

HOT TUBS

Originally, hot tubs were created from old wine barrels to re-create the experience of soaking in natural hot springs. Today's hot tubs serve essentially the same function, but they are made from a combination of fiberglass and acrylic plastics or from extruded thermal plastics. Molded shells are enclosed in a solid surround made of redwood, cedar, or teak to replicate the rustic wooden look. These tubs are extremely strong and are available in a variety of contours, colors, surface patterns, and textures.

Larger and deeper than whirlpools, hot tubs usually are purchased with a different philosophy in mind—socializing. They can be located outdoors on patios, decks, roofs, or near a backyard swimming pool. Or, they may be placed indoors in bedrooms, family rooms, basements,

or four-season porches—any location conducive to a relaxing soak with friends and family. When installing hot tubs indoors, you must measure to ensure they will fit through conventional entryways.

Portable hot tubs are soft-sided and made with marine-grade vinyl. These tubs are easy to set up—just fill them from a garden hose and plug the pump and motor into an appropriate electrical outlet. Some lightweight portables can be moved in and out of the house with the seasons. If you move, you can take them with you.

True 110v models don't always maintain water temperature when the jets are going full blast. You won't have this problem with 220v units, but they need special wiring.

Photo courtesy of PDC Spas

A portable hot tub takes up little space but offers room for three or more people. This model can be installed indoors or on your patio, and you can take it with you if you move.

The natural wood surround of this outdoor tub is reminiscent of the original hot tubs made from old wine barrels.

Custom-designed concrete tubs offer homeowners the opportunity to explore unconventional layouts such as this "mountain" spring.

This portable hot tub, made of traditional redwood and acrylic materials, easily fits anywhere—on the deck, in the backyard, or even inside your home.

Hot Tubs

Most hot tubs are self-enclosed, which means the pump, motor, and other support equipment are enclosed inside the surround and attached to the spa itself. These tubs can be installed into almost any space—indoors or out. You can install hot tubs completely above ground, resting on a floor indoors or on a cement patio or wood deck outdoors.

You may also purchase models that can be partially sunk into the ground. Some tubs can be inset completely, making the tub almost flush with the floor or ground surface.

Concrete spa tubs are custom designed by professional pool installers. Often, they are connected to an in-ground pool. They can be formed in any design or size and can be covered in ceramic tile for a dramatic effect.

Photo courtesy of LATCO Products

A custom-built concrete spa tub offers exciting design possibilities. The circular shape of this one, outlined and highlighted with blue and black ceramic tiles that contrast dramatically against a pure white background, readily demonstrates the stunning potential of tile and concrete.

Skylights and sliding patio doors create a solarium for this indoor hot tub. A wicker chair and potted plants complete this greenhouse effect.

SPA TUB FEATURES

Some spa tubs incorporate various jet combinations for direct massage therapy. These clusters of jets are positioned to pinpoint various body parts, such as lumbar, neck, and shoulder areas. Variable controls allow you to adjust the speed and type of jet spray. Settings range from a hard, pulsating spray for muscle massage to a gentle, circulating spray for relaxation.

Molded or contoured seats are features of some spa tubs, while others offer bench seating. Lounger seats provide a contoured reclining area, allowing you to totally immerse your body to gently soothe and massage away strain. There are also chairs that allow you to enjoy a full-body massage and the ultimate sensation of hydrotherapy.

Examples of therapeutic seating found in spa tubs include contoured bucket seats designed to accommodate spa users of various heights and sizes. Shorter people are more comfortable in seats that position them higher in the tub, while taller people are able to enjoy the spa in deeper seats. Seats with a natural tilt are more comfortable and allow you to position your body better to maximize contact with the different type jet streams available.

Other accessories for spa tubs include: headrests, footrests, mood lights, grab bars, floating game boards, floating trays for snacks, and a variety of water toys.

Insulated covers are available, which help maintain heat and lower your utility bill in addition to providing year-round security and safety.

Sculpted seating adds built-in support in this whirlpool designed for two bathers.

Whirlpool tubs are available in a variety of shapes, sizes, and colors with options such as built-in armrests, neck pillows, and luxury metal trim.

Insulated covers are available for outdoor spas, providing warmth in cold weather and security year-round.

A top side control panel allows you to adjust spa heat, power, and filtration without leaving the water.

25

SWIM SPAS

Swim spas are a cross between a jetted spa and a swimming pool. They are perfect for those who want to include swimming as part of their daily workout, at a fraction of the cost and space required for a pool.

Slightly larger than an average jetted spa tub, swim spas have powerful jets that create a current of rushing water to swim against. This current serves as a treadmill that moves you backward as you start swimming against it. You can adjust the rate of the current from that of a leisurely swim to a brisk workout.

Many swim spas double as conventional jetted spas, with a jetted massage area in one end with seating room for six and a swim area with main jets at the other. Simply turn up the temperature and adjust the current to transform the swim spa into a soothing massage therapy spa for guests.

Some larger models are installed at ground level, while others are freestanding units. The molded shells can run up to ten feet in width and twenty feet in length.

Photo courtesy of Cal Spas

A bird's-eye view of a freestanding swim spa shows the jets that create a current for the user to swim against. This model is only a little longer than an average-size person.

Set in an expansive atrium, this swim spa offers year-round exercise and relaxation.

DESIGN AND FUNCTION OF SPA TUBS

Spa tub jets recirculate water through a filter and a heater, using a pump. Together, the pump, the filter, and the heater make up the spa's support system.

Jets in larger hot tubs can number between nine and twenty-one. A typical hot tub has one primary high-volume jet, several fixed jets, several adjustable jets, and at least one back-massage jet.

Different types of jets provide specific and varied massage effects focused on particular muscles or muscle groups. Some tubs have jets positioned in clusters or combined to accentuate and enhance the therapy. The position of all jets is strategically matched to the contour of individual seating or therapy stations within the spa, ensuring that each jet or jet cluster is focused properly on its intended muscle or muscle group while providing you with the most comfortable environment to receive your therapy.

Pumps move the water around the tub by sucking it out of the tub and circulating it through the filtering and heating units and into the tub again. Most pumps are ¾ to 2 horsepower. One-speed and two-speed pumps are available, along with systems that have two separate pumps. Pumps are made of bronze, brass, and various types of plastic. The difference in price among the plastic pumps depends on the quality of the plastic. Bronze and brass pumps are more expensive, but they usually last much longer.

Heaters are powered either by natural gas or propane, electricity, or solar power. Heating costs in your area and how quickly you want the water to heat will determine which heater you choose. Whirlpool tubs don't require heaters because they rely on your home plumbing.

Photo courtesy of Kohler Co.

Clustered jets provide the ultimate massage effect for backs, necks, or even feet.

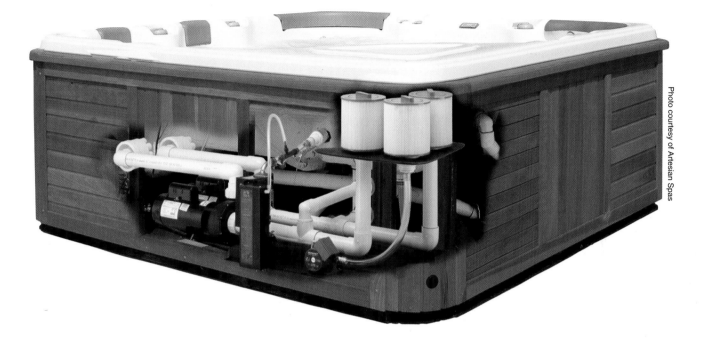

A cutaway view above shows the internal structure of a typical hot tub—pump, filters, and heater. The cross section below reveals jet placement, seat contours, and wall structure.

SUPPORT AND MAINTENANCE FOR SPA TUBS

Filters remove solid waste such as dirt, algae, and other residues that accumulate in the water. Three types of filters accomplish this. The cartridge filter, the most widely used filter in jetted spa tubs, allows water to pass through a cartridge while trapping foreign matter. The cartridge is easy to remove and clean.

There are also nonchemical options for filtering your spa. One alternative to standard filters is the ozonator, which purifies the water by feeding ozone gas into the water. The ozone gas kills most waterborne organisms on contact. Another nonchemical option is an ionizer, which kills organisms through an ion-exchange process. Both devices reduce the need for chemicals by 90%.

Water in hot tubs must be treated with chemicals to maintain the correct pH balance and to kill germs. Several manufacturers offer kits that contain all the necessary chemicals to sanitize your tub.

Photo courtesy of PDC Spas

Spa tub pumps propel water and air through jets and draw water through the tub's filter.

Photo courtesy of Watkins Manufacturing Corp.

Covers for hot tubs provide insulation and safety.

An ozonator mechanically sanitizes spa tubs by feeding ozone gas into the water, which kills most organisms. This sanitization method can reduce the need for chemical treatment.

Photo courtesy of Cal Spas

Elements of a Home Spa

SAUNAS

Saunas are part of an ancient tradition that has become a daily routine for many people. They're also a pleasant way to enhance physical and mental health. Saunas are ideal for reducing muscular stress, relieving congestion, revitalizing sore muscles, and stimulating circulation. Adding a sauna to your home spa lets you sweat out the day's tension in comfort and privacy.

Other beneficial effects of saunas include cleansing the complexion, relaxation, and reviving muscles after vigorous workouts. Saunas also stimulate circulation, enhance mental alertness, sharpen the senses, and relieve the symptoms of minor colds and illnesses. Saunas are even prescribed by health professionals as a way to relieve everyday aches and pains and aid in the treatment of joint problems.

First developed in Finland, saunas usually are built of soft aromatic woods such as cedar, redwood, or white spruce—porous woods that easily absorb and eliminate moisture. Saunas are heated by hot volcanic rocks, which in turn are heated by a radiant air heater. The heated air is circulated through intake and outlet vents that keep the humidity at less than 5%. Under these conditions, the body can tolerate temperatures up to 200° because perspiration evaporates almost immediately, causing an instant cooling effect.

You also can switch from a dry sauna to a steam bath by pouring a bit of water on the volcanic rocks. This makes the humidity quickly rise, shooting the temperature up for even more intense heat therapy. The steam adds moisture to the room and prevents the body from becoming too dehydrated.

To stimulate circulation, Finnish sauna bathers whisk their bodies with bundles of leafy birch twigs or pine boughs called vihtas. This light slap on the skin not only refreshes the mind and body, it also fills the room with the sweet scent of birch or pine.

A complete sauna consists of alternating heat and cold; bathers spend time in the hot stoveroom, then plunge into cold water. Saunas can last from one to three hours, alternating sessions of heat and cold, followed by a final washing-up session and time to relax in the after-sauna room. This room should be a quiet refuge where you relax and allow body temperature to slowly return to normal. A short nap or cup of hot tea or coffee can be a nice addition to this part of the sauna ritual.

The geometric window design on the entrance to this sauna adds drama and interest to the sauna experience.

Photo courtesy of Finnleo Sauna and Steam

Saunas range in size from those seating one or two to those that accommodate several people comfortably.

An atrium-style door opening only takes a little space while adding so much room.

Relaxing with friends and family in the sauna is a centuries-old Finnish tradition that detoxifies the body and rejuvenates the spirit.

Elements of a Home Spa

SAUNAS

A complete sauna can include four or five rooms or sections, depending on your preference. The stoveroom is at the heart of the sauna enclosure. When most people use the term *sauna*, they are referring to the stoveroom, the area that holds the hot volcanic rock. The rock is heated by a small stove fueled by wood, gas, or electricity. Water can be ladled on the hot rocks to produce steam. Besides the stoveroom, saunas can have a dressing area, a cold-water area, a relaxation room with kitchen facilities, and a supply room. To get the most from a total sauna experience, your home spa should include space for maximum pre-stoveroom preparation and post-stoveroom relaxation and cleansing.

The proportions of the stoveroom are critical to the sauna's performance. The proper combi-nation of heat and comfort requires that careful consideration be given to the total area available for the sauna, the number of bathers you want to accommodate at one time, the size of the stove, the amount and arrangement of bench space, the thickness of the insulation, and the size and position of the vents.

Since you don't do much walking around in the stoveroom, floor space is minimal. The best bench arrangements for saunas are either L- or U-shaped. An even simpler plan features a tiered bench that runs along one wall. The two or three levels allow areas of greater and lesser heat intensity. Benches should be wide enough for bathers to comfortably recline. A good rule of thumb for sauna benches is about 24 inches for each seated bather.

Standard sauna accessories include thermometer, wood bucket, wood ladle, headrest, backrest, and duck boards for walking on in front of the benches.

Clean, contemporary lines, along with the dry heat of the sauna, soothe and calm the day's anxieties. Modern furniture with a natural wood finish complements the wood panels of the sauna, making this an inviting place to rest and relax. Natural fabrics and neutral-colored tile complete the effect.

ENCLOSURES AND STEAM BATHS

Steam baths, steam cabinets, and environmental enclosures are other elements to consider including in your home spa. Steam rooms or baths offer health benefits similar to those in a sauna. Both cleanse the body from inside out by sweating out toxins. Steam bathing stimulates the skin and immune system as well.

Steam baths increase muscle suppleness and create a deep sense of relaxation. Steam cabinets keep the head cool, offering one of the most comfortable forms of steam bathing.

Steam baths are an essential part of the sauna experience. Toss water on the sauna's heated stones to envelope the sauna enclosure in moist heat. Alternating the sauna's dry heat with the moist steam bath completes the sauna ritual.

Cool marble lines the walls of this shower enclosure. A marble bench seat allows you to sit comfortably while showering or steam bathing.

ENCLOSURES AND STEAM ROOMS

Imagine enjoying a hot, dry desert breeze one minute and a steamy rain forest the next. Health environment enclosures offer an opportunity to enjoy a variety of different climates in the comfort of your own home. You can customize each session for temperature, duration, aromas, face, air, body, weight, and more. The enclosure offers health and wellness enhancement elements like deep back heating for relaxation and pain relief, dry sauna to soothe muscles, and adjustable massage therapy. You can create a mini-atmosphere for relaxation.

Photo courtesy of Finnleo Sauna and Steam

Bench seating allows you to stretch out in a multipurpose shower/steam room enclosure.

Photo courtesy of Kohler Co.

The equivalent of a "vertical whirlpool," this ten-jet shower system is the perfect water massage for tired, aching muscles.

Sleek curves coupled with marble surround impart an aesthetic aura for this enclosure, which contains shower, steam bath, and hydromassage.

Just close the door of this ingenious spa to enjoy the benefits of steam therapy. Installation takes only minutes—the portable enclosure requires no plumbing or rewiring and sets up in minutes.

39

Elements of a Home Spa

SHOWER SYSTEMS

A cool shower is a welcome refreshment before, after, and during a hot sauna. Today's showers have evolved into high-tech mini-spas that include pulsating body sprays, steam baths, and multiple shower heads.

If you desire, you can create a custom shower system that includes a steam generator for refreshing steam baths. Your spa can even include a luxury shower system with built-in seats, water cascades, and multijet mist systems.

Design your own shower environment with multifunction shower towers. The three-way shower head offers pulsating, full-flow, and soft-aerated sprays. Adjustable body sprays offer a variety of hydromassage effects with variable speeds, spray patterns, and water flow directions.

A multipurpose shower enclosure fits neatly atop a whirlpool bath in a conventional bathtub space.

This complete shower bath system integrates a luxury shower enclosure with a whirlpool bath.

Create your own luxurious shower experience with customized shower heads, body sprays, and interchangeable personal hand showers with varied spray patterns.

Elements of a Home Spa

SHOWER SYSTEMS

There's no limit to the number of shower heads you can install; therefore, there's no limit to the kind of custom shower you can create.

You can find shower systems with steam generators for refreshing steam baths while others have luxury showers with water cascades and a multijet mist system. Shower systems that aim jets at the head, neck, and other areas of tired, aching muscles are also available.

Another option you might want to consider for comfort and safety is seating. Seats are sometimes built in as an integral part of one-piece showers or custom-built shower stalls.

Multiple shower jets allow you to adjust flow for a custom water massage.

Combination whirlpool bath and glass shower tower provide optimal hydrotherapy and convenient showering all in one impressive system.

Combining the technology of a whirlpool bath and the comfort of a luxury shower, this high-tech shower system includes hydrotherapy jets, a cascading waterfall, and cleansing steam.

SUNLIGHT AND SUNTANNING SYSTEMS

If you live in a climate that experiences the full change of seasons, you'll appreciate and understand the importance of sunlight therapy. Artificial sunlight systems that deliver antidepressant effects for sufferers of seasonal affective disorder are also used for eating disorders, jet lag, insomnia, sleep disorders, and PMS. Specialized lights are available to promote enhanced levels of relaxation and deep sleep.

Tanning beds offer a healthy alternative to exposure to natural sunlight. There are many models available, from beds you can lie down on, pulling a cover across your body, to stand-up units that wrap around you and tan you while you're standing. Small tanning lamps that tan the face alone also are available.

Photo courtesy of ETS, Inc.

A tabletop face-tanning lamp offers tanning convenience for those on the go. It's handy, portable, and easy to store.

Photo courtesy of ETS, Inc.

Tan comfortably and conveniently in the privacy of your home by adding a tanning bed to your home spa.

An innovative alternative to conventional tanning beds, this fully adjustable canopy unit is easy to use and stores flat against a wall or slides into a closet.

A variety of lotions, gels, oils, and tanning intensifiers are available to enhance your tanning session.

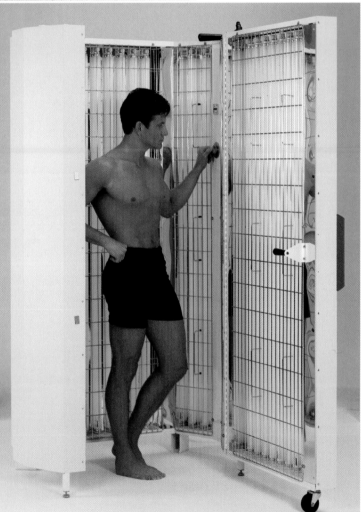

An enclosed booth amplifies tanning power for shorter tanning sessions and all-around results with no surface body contact.

EXERCISE EQUIPMENT

Even if space is limited, many exercise equipment products are specifically manufactured for use in small spaces. If you have only a small space to work with, consider machines that are compact, require little space to use, and can be collapsed and folded for out-of-the-way storage.

The type of exercise equipment you choose to include in your home spa depends on your personal preference and training regimen. Some people focus on high muscle definition, while others want increased muscle strength and flexibility. Many different fitness goals can be achieved with just a few different types of equipment.

There are many exercise machines on the market today, so some research is required to identify the equipment that best suits your workout needs. Some of the most popular exercise equipment today includes stationary bikes, treadmills, rowing machines, stair steppers, and nordic skiers, with new innovations arriving on the market every day. A little bit of research will help you identify the optimal features for each type of machine. For example, stationary bikes should have adjustable resistance controls on the handlebars so you can adjust tension while still pedaling. The seat should be comfortable and its height adjustable.

Home spa exercise areas should include enough equipment to give you a total body workout. Single-purpose machines are good for working one specific part of the body and are designed to be used with other machines to achieve a complete workout. Machines like stationary bikes and treadmills work your leg muscles. Free weights and rowing machines work on arm muscles. Some equipment, such as ski machines, provides a total body workout.

Photo courtesy of NordicTrack, Inc.

Enjoy the health benefits of cross-country skiing year-round with an indoor skier exercise machine.

Multifeatured, space-saving equipment is a popular choice for home spas. The design and features of this compact machine provide a full-body strength-training workout.

Elements of a Home Spa

EXERCISE EQUIPMENT

A multi-gym machine is a convenient choice that offers multiple machine options on one versatile machine. A multi-gym home fitness center can be as elaborate or as simple as you desire. Some features of a multi-gym include a handlebar for bench presses, squats, leg presses, and chin-ups. The machine can be adjusted easily to accommodate leg pull-down exercises and arm pulls. More elaborate machines include an extension bar for working the upper back and triceps and a low pull bar for arm curls or leg lifts.

Indoor treadmills allow you to enjoy a daily jog without worrying about the weather. Tread-mills build stamina and endurance in addition to burning calories. Many treadmills can be inclined to increase the aerobic workout.

Nordic ski machines use a pulling action that involves both arms and legs in the workout. These machines are easier on your bones and joints than treadmills.

Free weights are the cheapest and easiest way to equip your home spa. Free weights take up little room and can be stored easily when not in use. Your initial set should include an assortment of dumbbells for one-hand lifts, a 5-foot weight bar with a set of weight plates, and two collars to secure the weights.

Photo courtesy of NordicTrack, Inc.

Photo courtesy of NordicTrack, Inc.

Tone, shape, and define your body while burning calories with strength-training workout equipment.

The climber/stepper exercise machine simulates rock climbing and gives you a total body workout.

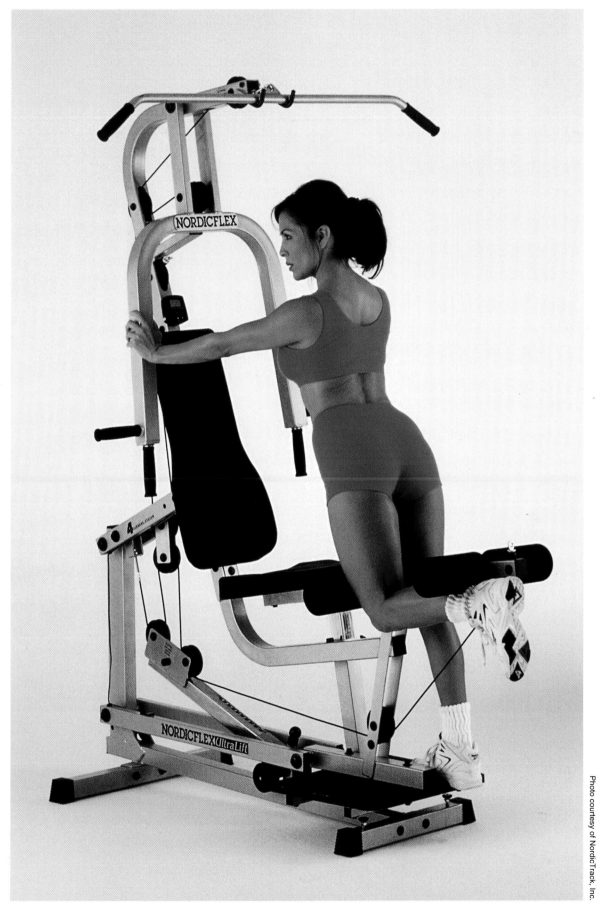

This health-club-quality machine uses pulleys and the user's body weight to provide total-body strength-training workouts.

SAFETY

Before you engage in the spa activities mentioned in this book, you should be aware of a number of safety precautions.

High temperatures create special safety considerations when dealing with heated tubs, saunas, and steam baths. People with heart problems, diabetes, and high blood pressure, and those on medications such as tranquilizers, antihistamines, and antibiotics, should consult a physician before entering a spa or taking a sauna. Pregnant women should never use saunas and spa tubs.

Be careful not to spend too much time in the tubs or sauna; soaking or staying in the sauna too long can raise your body heat beyond healthy levels. And be careful not to take a hot soak before you engage in strenuous activity. Muscles will be out of tone following hot-water soaking.

Never let children soak without adult supervision. Keep spa tubs covered when not in use to prevent anyone, especially a child, from accidentally falling in.

Sauna doors should swing outward to space outside the stoveroom and should never have a lock or latch that might trap someone inside.

In showers and next to spa tubs, install grab bars for safety. You may also want to install nonslip varieties of tile that offer a less slippery floor and reduce the risk of falling.

Tough, nonslip vinyl interlocking mats not only allow you to exercise safely by reducing exercise equipment vibration, they also protect your floors and carpet.

Grab bars make it safer and easier to get in and out of whirlpools; they are especially useful if youngsters or older adults will be using the tub. Grab bars mounted inside a whirlpool tub are options that must be specified when you order your tub. You can also buy grab bars designed to be mounted on the walls surrounding your whirlpool.

Sauna doors should swing out from the sauna interior so those inside can exit safely.

A PORTFOLIO OF
HOME SPA
IDEAS

RELAXATION SPAS

Go beyond the conventional to create atmosphere in your relaxation spa. Soft lights, muted colors, and soft, comfortable seats are elements you might want to consider for a relaxation spa. A relaxation spa is a place to pamper your mind and your body. It may be as simple as soaking in a sweetly scented tub or lounging in an innovative massage chair after a long day at the office or an intense workout. It is a place to relax and bring your body back to its normal temperature and pulse rate and a place to enjoy a soothing after-exercise soak.

An easy chair to curl up in with a good book or a cozy couch to catch a quick catnap allow you to stay in the same comfortable spot to enjoy a pleasant cooldown. Include a bookcase filled with favorite reading materials. You'll find that spending more time in your relaxation spa enhances your personal relaxation and reduces your stress level.

Choose tubs for relaxation that feature gentle curves, sloping backs, pillows, and armrests to enhance the comfort of your soaking experience.

A massage might be just what the doctor ordered for your relaxation spa. A number of massage machines that stimulate muscles and relieve stress and strain are available.

Tall windows frame a royal blue hot tub inset in creamy white tile, creating an oasis where you can unwind and escape your daily routine.

Shed the day's burdens in the warm, swirling water of a hot tub or whirlpool. The physical and pyschological benefits of a daily spa ritual are now well proven.

Photo courtesy of National Spa and Pool Institute

A private setting is ideal for a relaxation spa. A whirlpool tub in a master bathroom lets you conveniently escape the turmoil of the day.

Hot tubs can be enjoyed in any season, indoors or outdoors. Sharing the steamy, hot water with a friend is just the right antidote to a long winter's day. In addition to soothing tired muscles, a hot soak after a day on the slopes leaves you feeling both mentally and physically relaxed. For outdoor use in cool weather, most hot tubs can be fitted with insulated covers to conserve water heat when the tub is not in use.

Photo courtesy of HotSprings® Portable Spas, by Maximum Comfort Pool & Spas, Vail, CO.

(left) A circular tub looks down on the pool in this backyard, offering a relaxing soak after a vigorous swim or workout.

(below) Relax and enjoy quiet moments in a whirlpool or hot tub after a long day at the office or a hard workout at the gym.

Photo courtesy of National Spa and Pool Institute

Photo courtesy of PDC Spas

Share special moments with loved ones while relaxing in a hot tub, encircled by the soft glow of enchanting candlelight.

A whirlpool filled with warm, swirling water offers a place for solitude and reflection.

A comfy chair, fragrant blooms, and spa tub in a sunlit room create a quiet retreat from the daily routine.

63

The terra-cotta fireplace adjacent to this outdoor tub recalls a simpler time, setting the mood for a relaxing soak after a hectic day.

Photo courtesy of Finnleo Sauna and Steam

Whether basking in the gentle warmth of the sauna or in the warm mist of the steam bath, body and soul are refreshed and readied to take on the world. Cooling off in comfortable lounge chairs completes this relaxation ritual.

SOCIAL SPAS

Spas are areas that can bring people together to work off steam and to shed the pressures of a stressful day. Generally as large as any bedroom, social spas usually are located in common areas of the house, such as a porch, family room, basement, or outside on a deck or patio. Tubs for social spas can be large enough to hold as many as six bathers.

Families can enjoy the comforts of a large jetted tub to sit and soak together while discussing school, soccer, or the parts in the school play. These spas include large tubs with plenty of room for as many as six people to comfortably lounge and relax. Round, oval, and hourglass tubs are ideal shapes for social spa tubs.

A sauna is another spa element conducive to social interaction. Because minimal floor space is all that's needed in a sauna, social spa saunas should contain benches that are large enough for users to spread out and lie down.

Lively colors along with exciting patterns and visuals enhance the energy in a social spa. Ambience can also be created with equipment such as stereos, televisions, and video players for group workouts and entertainment while exercising.

Share the pain; workouts never seem as bad when you're doing them with others. When designing your social spa, don't forget fitness and exercise elements.

The finishing touch for your social spa is a comfortable after-exercise area where everyone can unwind and cool down after a spa, sauna, or exercise session. Include areas for changing and storing clothes, towels, and other accessories.

A backyard hot tub, large enough for several people, provides a place for family members to gather and share quality time while enjoying the benefits of water massage. Redwood steps match the wooden surround and allow easy access, even for the youngest family members.

Creating an atmosphere for entertaining friends in this spa tub requires little work. All you need is a lighted pathway, a solitary cactus, and the night desert air.

A four-season porch becomes a family "rec room" with a freestanding hot tub in the corner.

Photo courtesy of Patio Pools & Spas

Photo courtesy of Niles Audio Corp., Inc.

(right) A hot tub in a beautiful setting can be an ideal location for intimate social gatherings with a small group of people — or even just two. This custom ceramic hot tub with cascading fountain is sheltered by an overhead arbor and beautiful tropical garden.

(right) When you cook outdoors with your family or entertain the crowd from work, this gazebo-covered spa tub will be the centerpiece for any activity on this deck stretching across the backyard.

(below) A spacious tub inset in marble creates an elegant atmosphere for entertaining friends and neighbors.

Photo courtesy of HotSprings® Portable Spas by Georgio Assoc., Torrington, CT.

Photo courtesy of Marquis Spas

Children enjoy the swirling water of an outdoor hot tub and learn quickly that it is a great place to have fun with other family members. Children should, of course, be supervised when using a hot tub.

...sy of Mountain Hot Tub

A bridge spans the short distance to this spa tub, hidden from view by lush foliage and dense trees.

A redwood bridge crosses a backyard stream to this expansive deck, where guests move easily from the canopied hot tub to the shaded table nearby.

HOME SPAS FOR HEALTH BENEFITS

Imagine escaping to a warm, sunny beach, complete with a soothing ocean breeze, without leaving your house. A controlled-atmosphere system with artificial sunlight can make this a reality. Sunlight therapy is just one of the many innovative features you can include in your home spa to enhance your healthy lifestyle. Because spas provide stress relief and relaxation, almost every spa can be said to have health benefits.

Other home spa elements that promote a healthier lifestyle include saunas, jetted tubs, whirlpools, steam baths, tanning beds, and massage chairs.

The dry heat of the sauna relieves congestion, reduces stress, revitalizes sore, aching muscles, and stimulates respiration and circulation. Saunas also can improve body tone and help control weight. Just 20 minutes in a sauna can burn 300 to 600 calories!

Jetted tubs with many massaging jets offer other health benefits. Some tubs are available with special therapy seats that have different combinations of jets and hydrotherapeutic attributes. There are jets that create gentle, swirling water for rhythmic relaxation, while others stimulate and massage with vigorously pulsing water. Tubs are available with jets that can be directed at specific body points, such as the neck or lumbar area, for intense muscle relaxation therapy. Multijet combinations can be adjusted to focus on neck, foot, ankle, calf, knee, shoulder, or lumbar areas. These jets are found in molded seats contoured to fit comfortably around your body. Jetted spa tubs use a number of jets for various types of muscle relaxation.

Hydrotherapy is as good for the mind as it is for the body. There is almost no better way to melt away tension than a soak in a jetted spa tub. Relaxed muscles and reduced stress levels benefit those with high blood pressure, ulcers, and

For centuries, people have sought the healing waters of natural mineral hot springs. With an indoor whirlpool, you can have your own personal hot-water massage without leaving home.

nervous disorders. Relieving tension through hydrotherapy is also good therapy for arthritis and other bone and joint ailments.

Another way to relieve stress is through physical exertion. A healthy routine includes aerobic exercise as well as activity that builds and tones muscles. A home spa for health benefits includes equipment for both. Be sure there is enough room to use the equipment properly as well as a place to store equipment like weights, towels, and other smaller accessories.

Home spas that focus on improving your health also can include other health-related items such as scales that measure body mass and actual body fat.

And, as in any other room, the aesthetic atmosphere you create will enhance your level of relaxation. Soothing colors, gentle flowing music, and comfortable furniture all contribute to a more relaxed, healthier attitude.

Photo courtesy of NordicTrack, Inc.

A treadmill can provide exercise at any intensity level. Some models collapse for easy storage.

Photo courtesy of NordicTrack, Inc.

A daily exercise regimen increases flexibility, helps maintain weight, and increases total body strength. A good exercise device provides all three benefits.

Having exercise equipment in your own home gives you the opportunity to work at your leisure or when your schedule permits. If you can only include one type of exercise equipment in your home spa, choose one that works both your upper and lower body.

(left) Geometric patterns created by the wood paneling in a domed ceiling bestow a rustic, natural quality to this contemporary spa set in a splendid alcove.

(below) Don't have a lot of room for a combination spa? A small sauna, exercise bike, and lounge chair work well in this small space.

Photo courtesy of Finnleo Sauna and Steam

(right) Soaking in a whirlpool daily can relax sore muscles, reduce pain and stiffness, and let you manage daily activities with greater ease. A hand-held hydromassage attachment lets you isolate specific muscles.

(below) Hydrotherapy in a hot tub melts away the pain of arthritis, aching joints, and other stress-related ailments.

Strategically placed jets provide massage therapy for different parts of the body.

Regular sauna bathing can deep-clean the skin, promote weight loss, improve blood circulation, and induce a deeper, more relaxing sleep.

In today's fast-paced world, many people buy hot tubs for relaxation and to relieve stress. Soaking in a fresh-air spa tub amidst pleasant surroundings is a great way to beat stress and improve your overall well-being.

Photo courtesy of National Spa & Pool Institute

Warm-water massage is a gentle way for those with joint pain to reduce stress on affected joints, while increasing mobility.

COMBINATION SPAS

Imagine enjoying the benefits of a health club custom designed for you in the comfort and privacy of your own home. With the addition of a multifeatured combination spa, you'll never waste time commuting to the club or deal with increased membership dues ever again.

To get the most out of your home spa, it should be multifunctional. Combination spas offer the best of all worlds—a full line of exercise equipment, a sauna or steam room for healthy skin, and a soothing jetted tub for stress relief and muscle relaxation.

Many spas function as a combination of two or all three of the types described in this book: relaxation spas, social spas, and spas that are specifically designed to benefit your health.

The type of combination spa you choose to create can range from a small, tucked-away corner to an expansive, opulent retreat—depending on what best suits your budget and your needs. Another option is to build your combination spa over a period of time, adding equipment and features at your own pace.

A swim spa is an ideal feature for a combination space. These versatile spas can be set to provide a vigorous workout or a leisurely

A spa tub in your living room? There is no question this homeowner considers soaking in a hot tub to be an important part of the day. The living room centers around this tub, creating the ideal room for entertaining or just relaxing.

swim. Or, you can even turn them off altogether, raise the water temperature, and invite your neighbors over for a friendly dip.

Surprisingly, some of the better spas can be created in the most private of spaces—the bathroom. Bathrooms are a natural spot for a relaxing spa, of course, but exercise equipment can easily find a home in a bathroom. And, under the right circumstances, bathroom spas can allow for intimate socializing.

Photo courtesy of Andersen Windows, Inc.

This combination spa, created in an upstairs bathroom, features a whirlpool, rower, exercise cycle, and a scale.

Photo courtesy of Congoleum Corporation

The whirlpool and fitness cycle in this bathroom incorporate basic spa elements into an existing space.

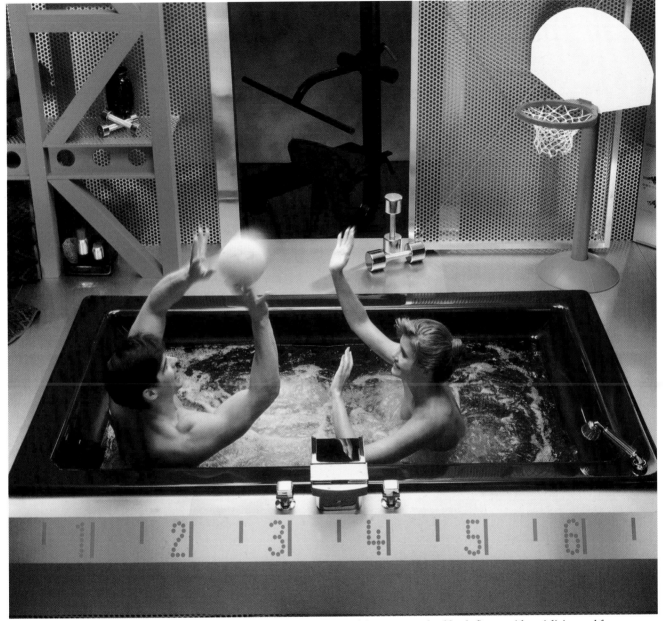

A whirlpool, exercise bench, free weights, and recreational games create a multipurpose spa that blends fitness with socializing and fun.

(right) A large hot tub placed near the dock and lake adds another dimension to your lakefront property.

(below) A tiled hot tub in a four-season porch serves as a focus point for a combination spa with room to add exercise equipment, lounge furniture, or a small sauna.

(right) Regardless of spa size, you can always include multipurpose lounge furniture, such as this massage chair that reclines at the touch of a button and soothes away tension and stress.

(right) A sunroom or solarium is well suited for a multifunction spa. Plentiful sunlight, potted plants, and an attractive view create a pleasant environment for exercising and relaxing.

(below) Tanning beds don't have to take up a lot of space. This unconventional unit is completely adjustable and folds away against a wall or inside a closet.

Photo courtesy of ETS, Inc.

A swim spa in your backyard is an excellent idea for those with limited backyard space. It takes up less room than a standard pool but provides the same health and recreational benefits.

(left) Nestled under open rafters, a traditional redwood hot tub makes a strong statement in a combination or multipurpose home spa, with plenty of room for exercising, relaxing, or just socializing with friends.

(below) An environmental steam bath enclosure with heat adds an extra dimension in any spa.

(right) Exercise equipment, a steam bath/shower, and a full sauna create a multipurpose spa where you can work out, relax, and rejuvenate your whole body.

(below) Adding tanning equipment to your home spa is easy with a stand-up wrap-around tanning booth.

Photo courtesy of ETS, Inc.